Welcome to the tribe for horseback adventure lovers.

If you love horses, travel and adventure, you'll find all you need on our website to have more adventures with your own horses or with other people's horses around the globe.

 SEE OUR LATEST BOOKS & POSCASTS

BOOKS

True horse stories of women having incredible adventures and overcoming amazing odds while riding horses in exotic places.

PODCAST

Listen to over 250+ Episodes for free on iTunes, Spotify, Stitcher, Amazon Music and more.

WWW.EQUESTRIANADVENTURESSES.COM

FOLLOW OUR SOCIAL MEDIA   @EQUESTRIANADVENTURESSES

JOIN OUR FACEBOOK GROUP!

CONTENTS

How to Use this Book

VERIFIED BADGE

A Verified Badge is only given to stables which the Equestrian Adventuresses Team has personally visited and verified the welfare of the horses with their own eyes.

In the pages of this book you will find countless bucket list items from faraway lands. You can check these items off your list with our handy "checklist" found at the back of the book.

Remember to share this book with your friends and loved ones so that you can enjoy crossing these items off your list together! Post your photos of each bucket list item you are chasing (or completing!) inside our Facebook Group: Equestrian Adventuresses.

www.facebook.com/groups/equestrianadventuresses

LOOK OUT FOR THESE FOR FUN AND INTERESTING FACTS!

All Inclusive Horseback Riding Vacations

RANCHO LAS CASCADAS

rancholascascadas.com

imagine riding

www.imagineriding.com

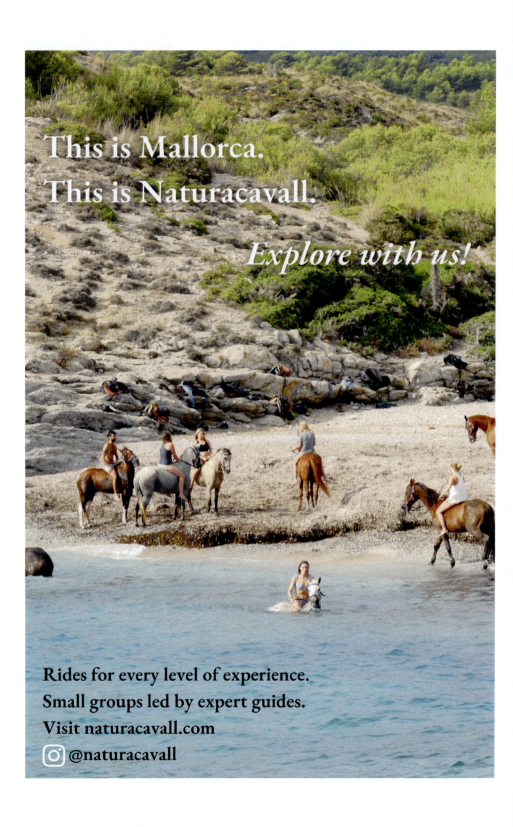

www.equestrianadventuresses.com

POD CAST

New Episodes Every Monday, Wednesday, Friday

AVAILABLE ON ALL PODCAST PLAYERS SUCH AS ITUNES, SPOTIFY, STITCHER, AMAZON MUSIC, AUDIBLE AND MORE...

UTE TONIA

HEATHER CALVERT

●LIVE

PODCAST TOPICS:

HORSEBACK TRAVEL, ADVENTURES, TIPS, INTERVIEWS, DESTINATION GUIDES

SECTION ONE
ADVENTURES WITH YOUR OWN HORSE

FUN TIPS, RESOURCES AND INSPIRATIONAL STORIES:
WWW.EQUESTRIANADVENTURESSES.COM

PRO TIP: LISTEN TO THE 18 DIFFERENT SPEAKER PRESENTATIONS FOUND IN THE "ADVENTURES ON HORSEBACK VIRTUAL WORKSHOP" TO HEAR FIRSTHAND THE MISTAKES LONG RIDERS MADE (AND WHAT THEY WOULD HAVE DONE DIFFERENTLY!) LISTEN TO SPEAKERS SUCH AS BERNICE ENDE "LADY LONG RIDER," CATHLEEN LEONARD (MEMBER OF THE LONG RIDER'S GUILD) AND MORE!

"COURAGE IS BEING SCARED TO DEATH BUT SADDLING UP ANYWAY." -JOHN WAYNE

Equestrian Adventuresses Bingo

Get 5 in a Row & Share your filled out Bingo Card in the Equestrian Adventuresses Facebook Group. Winners will win fabulous prizes!

Leave a Review on Amazon for Saddles & Sisterhood Book	Leave a Review on Amazon for Going the Distance Book	Leave a Review on Amazon for Leg Up Book	Leave a Review on Amazon for Have Breeches Will Travel Book	Post a photo of you and a horse in our Facebook Group
Leave a podcast review on iTunes	Subscribe to our podcast on iTunes	Follow us on Instagram	Leave a Review on Amazon for Going the Distance Book	Post a photo of you and one of our books in our Facebook Group
Post a photo of you and one of our books in our Facebook Group	Leave a Review on Amazon for Leg Up Book	Follow us on Instagram	Post an introduction in our Facebook Group	Leave a Review on Amazon for Saddles & Sisterhood Book
Leave a Review on Amazon for Going the Distance Book	Post a photo of you and a horse in our Facebook Group	Leave a Review on Amazon for Have Breeches Will Travel Book	Post a photo of you and one of our books in our Facebook Group	Subscribe to our Youtube
Subscribe to our Youtube	Leave a Review on Amazon for Saddles & Sisterhood Book	Like our Facebook Page	Post a photo of you and one of our books and tag us on Instagram	Leave a podcast review on iTunes

Prizes:
1 set: Equestrian Adventuresses Box Set Books 1-5
2 sets: Around the World on 180 Horses Book Series Books 1 & 2
3 Sets: FREE Lifetime Access to our Adventures on Horseback Virtual Workshop

Bring Your Own Horse

Explore The World Together

Take your trusted four-legged partner with you during your travel adventures.

BUCKET LIST #1:
RIDE IN A PARADE

All the people talking, whistling, and enjoying their day out in the town, watching you ride down the street. Show off your horse and represent your culture by riding in a parade.

BUCKET LIST #2:
DO AN OBSTACLE COURSE

Try a fun obstacle course with your trusted equine partner. This will be a great experience for children as well, so bring the whole family for adventurous day on horseback.

BUCKET LIST #3:
PLAY A GAME OF POLO

THIS GAME IS ONE OF THE WORLD'S OLDEST KNOWN TEAM SPORTS

DID YOU KNOW?

"'"WHEN THE ALMIGHTY PUT HOOFS ON THE WIND AND A BRIDLE ON THE LIGHTNING, HE CALLED IT A HORSE." - AUTHOR UNKNOWN

BUCKET LIST #4:
BIRD WATCHING ON HORSEBACK

The sounds of birds chirping is an excellent way to find peace and feel connected with nature. Bring a pair of binoculars and see if you can spot different birds on your ride out!

BUCKET LIST #5:
BUY A HORSE OF YOUR OWN

Every horse lover should own their own horse! Maybe rescue a horse and give a good home to a horse in need.

BUCKET LIST #6:
GO FOR A MULTI-DAY POINT TO POINT RIDE WITH YOUR HORSE

YOU CAN LEARN ABOUT HOW TO DO MULTI-DAY RIDES BY WATCHING THE "ADVENTURES ON HORSEBACK VIRTUAL WORKSHOP" ON:

WWW.EQUESTRIANADVENTURESSES.COM

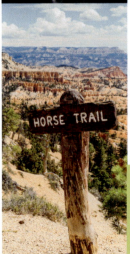

"STOP BEING AFRAID OF WHAT COULD GO WRONG, AND START BEING EXCITED OF WHAT COULD GO RIGHT"
– TONY ROBBINS

BUCKET LIST #7:

GALLOP THROUGH AN OPEN FIELD

It's a warm fall day, right when the leaves are turning colors. You are out for a quick ride around the farm and get to an open field. You and your horse are thinking the same thing- time for a nice, consistent gallop through the yellow grass

BUCKET LIST #8:

SPEND TIME GROOMING YOUR HORSE

BUCKET LIST #9:

BRAID/BAND YOUR HORSE'S MANE

BUCKET LIST #10:
TEACH YOUR HORSE LIBERTY

You and your horse are equal, feel the harmony you have together as you build a stronger bond by doing some groundwork and teaching them liberty. Make sure to give a lot of treats!

Start off in a small space and begin with simple tasks like moving away from a whip and following you around that space.

Bucket List #11: Go Swimming

Grab your bathing suit and cool off in a nearby river. Feel the weightlessness as the water carries you and your horse down the stream. The emerald-colored water will leave you feeling fresh for the rest of your ride.

Bucket List #12: Gallop Down A Track

Trumpets sounding... and their off. You probably will not be in the next Kentucky Derby, but you can race your own horse down the same track. Pushing your horse forward, feeling his stride stretching underneath you, feeling the air press against your face... you are free.

Bucket List #13: Enter A Horse Show

Go to a show and enter a few classes that you think you and your horse would enjoy. Practice a bit before the date and go in there and show them what you got! No matter if you come out with first or tenth, it will be a great experience.

Bucket List #14: Try A New Discipline

If you already show, branch out and try a new discipline. This will keep your horse's mind engaged and give you something new to focus on. Plus, this is a great way to make new friends and see new places.

Bucket List #15: Attend A Clinic

Equestrians never stop learning. There is so much knowledge to be obtained about these complex creatures. Attending a clinic will give you more insight about your horse and will help you with your riding.

Bucket List #16: Go Camping

The sky is filled with stars, you hear owls in the distance, and there is a fresh aroma of a campfire. Your horse just ate his dinner and is staked out in the tree line; you're eating smores and thinking about what trail you will take in the morning. Camping is the perfect getaway for you and your horse.

Bucket List #17: Ride Without A Bridle

Anticipating your horse's movements, driving your seat into the saddle, connecting with them deeper than you ever have. Riding without a bridle is a great accomplishment to gain with your horse.

Bucket List #18: Ride Bareback

Riding bareback is such a fun thing to do. There is barely any prep; just go to an open pasture and ride freely. Plus, it will make your leg muscles stronger.

BUCKET LIST #19:
TEACH YOUR HORSE TO PULL A BUGGY

A crack of a whip, the sound of wheels moving on the pavement, your making you way to the nearby market. But instead of being in a car, you took your horse and buggy.

Just like the olden days when the form of transportation was horses. How cool would it be to hook up your trusty steed and ride down the road?

FORGET THE CARS, YOU HAVE REAL HORSEPOWER

BUCKET LIST #20:
RIDE TO A PUB OR RESTAURANT

Have a drink or meal while your horse stands nearby.

BUCKET LIST #21:
RIDE TO A WATERFALL

Load your horse up and head out to a National Park and spend the day riding to a waterfall.

SECTION TWO
HORSEBACK TOURS AND RIDING VACATIONS

FUN TIPS, RESOURCES AND INSPIRATIONAL STORIES: WWW.EQUESTRIANADVENTURESSES.COM

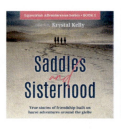

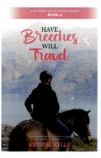

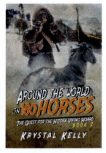

PRO TIP: BRING A BOOK TO READ ON THE FLIGHT, ON RAINY DAYS, OR TO HELP INSPIRE YOU FOR YOUR NEXT ADVENTURE! READ INCREDIBLE TRUE STORIES OF EQUESTRIAN ADVENTURESSES ON AMAZON WORLDWIDE OR LISTEN TO THE AUDIO BOOKS ON AUDIBLE.

"THE ESSENTIAL JOY OF BEING WITH HORSES IS THAT IT BRINGS US IN CONTACT WITH THE RARE ELEMENTS OF GRACE, BEAUTY, SPIRIT, AND FREEDOM." - SHARON RALLS LEMON

imagine riding

It's time to
VACATION

ALL INCLUSIVE STAY

CONTACT US

WWW.RANCHOLASCASCADAS.COM

RIDE THROUGH DIFFERENT TERRAINS

#22: Mountains

Ride through the rocky tracks up a mountain to watch the sunset at the peak. It will give you the perfect opportunity for an awesome camping trip before you head back down.

Ride in Vermont with Kimberly Farms: www.KimberlyFarms.org

#23: Desert

Nothing is like feeling the soft sand under your horse's hooves as he walks over large sand dunes.

Ride in Egypt with Horses & Hieroglyphs: www.horsesandhieroglyphs.com

#24: Beach

Galloping down the coast, feeling the fresh breeze on your face, the sound of your horse's hooves hitting the wet sand...

RIDE THROUGH DIFFERENT TERRAINS

#25: Castles

One of the best thing about riding horses in Europe is riding in medieval cities to castles!

Ride in France with Touraine Cheval:

https://tourainecheval.com

#26: Villages

It's a unique experience riding into a remote village on horseback. In many of these hard to reach places you will hardly see any tourists or travelers and you will get treated like an intrepid adventuress by the locals. (Most likely invited inside for tea!)

Ride in Egypt with Horses & Hieroglyphs:
www.horsesandhieroglyphs.com

RIDE THROUGH DIFFERENT TERRAINS

#27: Jungles & Forests

Ancient forests, wildlife, flora and fauna and various animals have never looked better than from between the horses' ears. Riding in Yosemite National Park, the Jungles of Asia or the forests of Europe... you can't go wrong.

#28: Rivers

Crossing a river on horseback is a right of passage it seems. Many destinations offer a variety of experiences from small to big rivers.

#29: Canyons

Arizona on mules, New Mexico, Kazakhstan, Jordan and other destinations offer gorgeous canyon rides from horseback.

RIDE THROUGH DIFFERENT TERRAINS

#30: Steppes

In Mongolia you'll find vast expanses of valleys and plains known as the "steppes." If you want to know what it feels like to ride without fences, this is the place!

#31: Marshes

In the Camargue in France and Connemara in Ireland as well as Dartmoor in the United Kingdom, you can experience "marsh land." Just be careful not to stray from the trail!

#32: Glaciers & Snow

Iceland and Greenland are excellent places to see iceburgs from horseback. Norway and Canada are other great spots for rides in the snow.

Adventures on Horseback Virtual Workshop

The first and ONLY virtual event with equestrian speakers and presenters from around the globe brought together in one space to share their horseback adventure tips, secrets and their biggest mistakes and lessons learned!

https://bit.ly/eqa-workshop

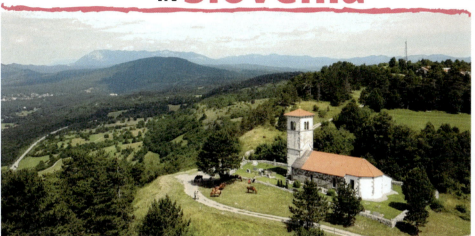

BUCKET LIST #33:

RIDE TO LUXOR IN EGYPT

Luxor: this is where you will see the many fabled temples and tombs scattered along the banks of the Nile. It is also where you will ride a swift and elegant Arabian horse through every terrain, from lush sugar plantations and banana groves to palm-fringed lanes and open desert plains. You will discover a simple and peaceful place where traditional feluccas still sail quietly back and forth along the river.

All this against the backdrop of the astonishing 'open-air-musem' of Luxor.

BOOK A TOUR OF EGYPT ON HORSEBACK WITH IMAGINE RIDING. VISIT: WWW.IMAGINERIDING.COM

"LIFE IS A JOURNEY, NOT A DESTINATION."
- RALPH WALDO EMERSON

BUCKET LIST #34:

CANTER THROUGH FIELDS OF FLOWERS

Canter through fields thick with jewel-toned flowers reaching up to your horse's chest. Inhale the sweet scents carried through the warm mountain air and revel in the verdant paradise of our Cactus Flowering Season – one of the many gifts bestowed by our Eternal Spring climate.

BOOK A TOUR IN MEXICO WITH RANCHOS LAS CASCADAS. VISIT: WWW.RANCHOLASCASCADAS.COM

BUCKET LIST #35:

SWIM WITH HORSES AT DAWN FROM A SECRET BEACH

Ride the wild, secret beaches and rocky coast of Llevant on the East coast of Mallorca, Spain. Ride a horse into the beautiful turquoise waters of the Mediterranean Sea. Later you can dine out at a stunning mountain restaurant with panoramic views. Your bed for the night is a hammock in a remote forest, lit only by the moon. Rest amongst the wild pine and juniper trees far from civilisation.In the morning, rise at dawn, and ride down to the sea for another swim with the horses before breakfast and a few more hours soaking up nature on horseback. Gallop along long white sandy stretches of beach and through cool forests.

BOOK A TOUR IN BEAUTIFUL MALLORCA ISLAND WITH NATURA CAVALL. VISIT: HTTPS://NATURACAVALL.COM/

"DO NOT FOLLOW WHERE THE PATH MAY LEAD. GO INSTEAD WHERE THERE IS NO PATH AND LEAVE A TRAIL" - RALPH WALDO EMERSON

RIDE IN A FESTIVAL IN INDIA

This ride was specifically developed for Imagine Riding. The place is Malwa, South-East Rajasthan: lush fields, dotted with villages, small palaces, old hill forts and beautifully ad-orned farmhouses.

A region traditional in character and appearance and undis-turbed by tourism,

The ride takes place during Navratri, a nine-day festival dev-oted to the worship of Goddess Durga. We will be able to take part in local festivities.

BOOK A TOUR OF INDIA ON MARWARI HORSES WITH IMAGINE RIDING. VISIT: WWW.IMAGINERIDING.COM

"OH THE PLACES YOU'LL GO." - DR. SEUSS

BUCKET LIST #37:
RIDE OFF THE BEATEN TRACK

For a day, for a night, for up to a week, whatever time frame you have, you will truly feel free when you ride in rural Mallorca. Get off the beaten track, forget your troubles and just be in the moment with your horse. Mallorca has many unspoilt spots only known to the cowboys of Naturacavall so put yourself in their capable hands. Sleep overnight in a tipi on comfy sleeping mats and cushions, after eating dinner cooked outside on the open fire. Enjoy the smell of wood smoke in your hair, and the feel of the dirt under your nails.

BOOK A TOUR IN BEAUTIFUL MALLORCA ISLAND WITH NATURA CAVALL. VISIT: HTTPS://NATURACAVALL.COM/

MALLORCA ISLAND IS THE LARGEST ISLAND IN ALL OF SPAIN.

DID YOU KNOW?

BUCKET LIST #38:
RELAX AT AN EQUESTRIAN RETREAT

Create your own post-ride ritual with a freshly-made margarita by our infinity pool whilst the sun sets over the highlands. Or perhaps give your favorite steed a relaxing grooming session before heading to the muscle-soothing comfort of our jacuzzi, overlooking our very own waterfall, pina colada in hand.

BOOK A TOUR IN MEXICO WITH RANCHOS LAS CASCADAS. VISIT:
WWW.RANCHOLASCASCADAS.COM

POINT TO POINT RIDE

This one of kind ten-day journey has only been done twice before on horseback. It is a camping expedition with a backup team looking after all of our needs as we follow these historic and eerily beautiful paths. It is an adventure of a lifetime.

"I am not the same, having seen the moon shine on the other side of the world" – Mary Anne Radmacher

BUCKET LIST #39:
RIDE IN TURKEY

Ride along the ancient tracks that crisscross this valley. We travel through ever-changing scenery. Rock hewn temples and ancient burial tombs are scattered throughout. Strange volcanic rock formations and fairy chimneys line our path. Ever onwards we ride alongside riverbanks, lakes and on forests ways once crossed by the caravans, kings and armies of ancient times. Turkish Arabian and Arabian cross endurance horses, fit and forward-going are our reliable steeds.

BUCKET LIST #40:
GALLOP THROUGH ANCIENT VINYARDS BEFORE DINING OUT AT SUNSET AMONGST THE VINES

Learn about wine, how it is grown, and how it is made, appreciate the craft and the time it takes to create a vintage, and then try it for yourself, right where it was grown! The quality of Mallorca's wine production is exemplary and the Macia Batle vineyard is internationally famous for its wine. Ride through the private grounds of the ancient vineyards, arriving at sunset to drink and dine in style. A feast for the soul, mind and body!

BOOK A TOUR IN BEAUTIFUL MALLORCA ISLAND WITH NATURA CAVALL. VISIT: HTTPS://NATURACAVALL.COM/

MOUNTAINS AND SEA

Cook on an open fire whilst the horses rest and graze around you. Ride on the following day towards the spectacular coastline of the island, where the sand is pure and the water is a bright turquoise blue.

MONESTARIES

Ride through historic towns and country lanes to discover a monastery where you can sleep where the monks once did.

BUCKET LIST #41:

EXPLORE A UNESCO HERITAGE SITE

Ride through the rural Mallorcan countryside and stay overnight in an eco-finca completely disconnected from the outside world. Ride to the sea, monasteries and more. Stay overnight this time in a local ranch where the locals are very friendly. Finally, descend back down through the mountains where the eagles soar through the extraordinary UNESCO protected world heritage Tramuntana mountains.

BUCKET LIST #42:
ENJOY A PICNIC WITH HORSES

Join us in El Fresno for a surprise picnic at one of our favorite local spots. Sip tequila from horseback as we welcome you to an authentic home-cooked Mexican picnic, set beside the waterfalls and crystal-clear streams of our local cascades. After your al-fresco dining experience why not enjoy a refreshing dip in the sparkling waters, or take a siesta under the shade of a Weeping Willow.

**BOOK A TOUR IN MEXICO WITH RANCHOS LAS CASCADAS. VISIT:
WWW.RANCHOLASCASCADAS.COM**

BUCKET LIST #43:

RIDE ON CRIOLLO HORSES WITH AUTHENTIC MEXICAN CHARROS AS YOUR GUIDE

Experience the freedom of truly unrestricted riding on our all-day trail to the mysterious Los Organos stones. Gallop through remote winding canyons lined with towering cacti, home only to wild horses and soaring eagles. With scenery straight from a Wild West movie, it's a thrilling adventure your inner Cowgirl or boy will never forget.

BOOK A TOUR IN MEXICO WITH RANCHOS LAS CASCADAS. VISIT: WWW.RANCHOLASCASCADAS.COM

69 DIFFERENT LANGUAGES ARE SPOKEN IN MEXICO

DID YOU KNOW?

"IF I HAD ASKED PEOPLE WHAT THEY WANTED, THEY WOULD HAVE SAID FASTER HORSES."
– HENRY FORD

RIDE WITH NATURA CAVALL

https://naturacavall.com/

RIDE ON THE GREEN WAY

Discover " La Via Verde - the green way". These are disused train tracks which have been repurposed for horses and hikers.

"Stay away from a horse long enough and you'll start tapping your fingers to the beat of a trot."
– Unknown

RIDE UNDER THE MOONLIT SKY

The "Via Verde" 30km track is ideal for long stretches of galloping through stunning countryside. Stop off along the way at the old station house restaurant for some typical local food. After refreshing yourself, and your horse, continue on through the evening across tracks, fields and country lanes before reaching a remote country house. Finish your day with a meal around the campfire before retiring for the night to a cosy bed. The following day ride back with stunning coastal views, and the seawind in your hair and your horse's mane.

RIDE TO A VOLCANO IN ECUADOR

Not only will we ride with Chagra cowboys in the Ecuadorian Highlands but we will also follow their work as they roundup their livestock and share with us their lifestyle, traditions and horsemanship. Ride through the mountains and valleys of the Ecuadorian highlands. Riding home-bred trekking horses we move from point to point staying in remote working haciendas. From the subtropical montagne Cloud Forests we head towards higher altitude with its rocky volcanic landscapes, passing volcanoes and climbing mountain ridges.

BOOK A TOUR IN ECUADOR WITH IMAGINE RIDING. VISIT: WWW.IMAGINERIDING.COM

"DO NOT FOLLOW WHERE THE PATH MAY LEAD. GO INSTEAD WHERE THERE IS NO PATH AND LEAVE A TRAIL" - RALPH WALDO EMERSON

BUCKET LIST #46:
SEE THE BUTTERFLY MIGRATION FROM HORSEBACK

Ride through the ancient fir forests of Central Mexico and bear witness to the Monarch Butterfly migration - one of the natural world's most wonderous spectacles. Feel an intimate connection with the pure magic of Mother Nature as you gaze upon millions of Monarchs filling the air with flashes of crimson beauty.

BOOK A TOUR IN MEXICO WITH RANCHOS LAS CASCADAS. VISIT: WWW.RANCHOLASCASCADAS.COM

TRAVEL+LEISURE MAGAZINE SAYS: "WITNESSING THE MONARCH BUTTERFLY MIGRATION IN MEXICO SHOULD BE ON EVERY NATURE-LOVER'S BUCKET LIST."

"DATE SOMEONE WHO SPOILS YOU LOVES YOU RESPECTS YOU, AND NEVER QUESTIONS HOW MUCH YOU SPEND ON YOUR HORSES."
– UNKNOWN

BUCKET LIST #47:
RIDE TO AN ANCIENT TEMPLE

Ride horses in Bhutan, Tibet, Nepal, Indonesia or China. Learn about Buddhist culture, drink the butter milk tea, and laugh with monks from horseback as you travel back in time to unknown places.

LISTEN TO THE EQUESTRIAN ADVENTURESSES PODCAST FOR MORE TIPS, DESTINATIONS AND INTERVIEWS OF STRONG EQUESTRIAN ADVENTURESSES!

BUCKET LIST #48:
RIDE IN A 'RAVAL' RACE AT BIBLICAL BALOTRA HORSE FAIR

There is nothing to beat the thrill of trotting your Marwari in 'Raval' (fast 4 paced trot) at speed and in competition with local rural riders on a dried up riverbed amidst the most biblical of Rajasthan's horse fairs with Horse India.

BOOK A HORSE RIDING HOLIDAY WITH HORSE INDIA. VISIT: HTTPS://WWW.HORSEINDIA.COM

BUCKET LIST #49:
RIDE IN FRANCE

We offer the opportunity to ride through enchanting villages, unspoilt woodland, following river valleys and gorges, and canter across fields. We have 26 horses, a variety of breeds, some home bred, to cover different weights, experience and confidence. All the rides have beautiful views and lovely canters.

BOOK A HORSE RIDING HOLIDAY IN FRANCE. VISIT: WWW.FRENCHRIDINGHOLIDAYS.CO.UK

BUCKET LIST #50:
EXPLORE EUROPE ON HORSEBACK

BOOK A HORSE RIDING HOLIDAY IN FRANCE. VISIT: WWW.FRENCHRIDINGHOLIDAYS.CO.UK

BUCKET LIST #51:
BINGE EAT GREEK FOOD WHILE YOUR HORSE IS TIED NEARBY

BOOK A HORSE RIDING HOLIDAY IN GREECE.
VISIT: WWW.IPPOSMOLYVOS.COM

BUCKET LIST #52:
RIDE ON AN ISLAND

BOOK A HORSE RIDING HOLIDAY IN GREECE.
VISIT: WWW.IPPOSMOLYVOS.COM

BUCKET LIST #53:
VISIT OLD FORTS ON HORSEBACK

Rajasthan is well-known for its forts and palace. Visit on horseback the impressive Kumbhalgarh Fort, part of the UNESCO World Heritage Site Hill Forts of Rajasthan or the ruin of the medieval Parsoligarh Fort and marvel at the ancient splendor and history of the maharajas.

BOOK A HORSE RIDING HOLIDAY IN INDIA. VISIT: HTTP://WWW.PRINCESSTRAILS.COM

BUCKET LIST #54: RIDE WITH A HERD OF HORSES

When we set off on a multi-day trip, each rider will have their horse, plus we take along several extra horses to change out and give others a rest if necessary.

The extra horses are special and can usually do double duty as a good riding horse and a good pack horse. We don't ride nose to tail, but it's a great feeling to move along together over the countryside.

BOOK A HORSE RIDING HOLIDAY WITH STONE HORSE MONGOLIA: WWW.STONEHORSEMONGOLIA.COM

France

BUCKET LIST #55:
RIDE WITH FELLOW EQUESTRIAN ADVENTURESSES

RIDE IN FRANCE WITH TOURAINE CHEVAL. VISIT: HTTPS://TOURAINECHEVAL.COM

RIDE IN VERMONT WITH KIMBERLY FARMS: WWW.KIMBERLYFARMS.ORG

Vermont

BUCKET LIST #56:
RIDE THROUGH THE AMAZING ANDES MOUNTAINS

Enjoy the marvelous nature views from the back of your horse: Snow Mountains, deep valley's, beautiful lakes and impressive rock formations. Donkeys and flocks of sheep and llama's crossing your path. Birds and crickets wake you up in the morning when the sun rises over the top of the mountains...

RIDE IN PERU. VISIT: WWW.HACIENDADELCHALAN.COM

Peru

"THERE ARE ONLY TWO EMOTIONS THAT BELONG IN THE SADDLE; ONE IS A SENSE OF HUMOR AND THE OTHER IS PATIENCE." - JOHN LYONS

MOUNTAINS AND SEA

Ride on one of the islands in Italy such as Sardinia or Sicily for a beach view. Or head north to the famous Dolomites Mountains and play snow polo or ride the rugged terrain.

ANCIENT CITIES

Learn all about how Hannibal crossed the Alps with Elephants to try to capture Rome.See Roman architecture and statues up close and in person. Marvel at the hilltop fortresses and castles.

DELICIOUS ITALIAN FOOD

After a long day touring Italy, grab a nice pasta dinner at a local restaurant or get a quick snack at a street pizza stand.

BUCKET LIST #57:
RIDE IN A MEDIEVAL CITY IN ITALY

A whistle from the breeze fills your ears as you ride down the narrow, dark allyway. It makes you notice the gorgeous gothic arcitecture on the glooming evening. Your in Periguia for the evening and are learning about the collapes of the roman empire and the italian renaissance.

BUCKET LIST #58: RIDE IN GREECE

There is something beautiful in this village that gives you a sense of relaxation. The hospitality and the laid back lifestyle of the locals pulls you in to join them and if that doesn't do it you can always go to the thermal baths to soak your body in natural warm waters.

**BOOK A HORSE RIDING HOLIDAY IN GREECE.
VISIT: WWW.IPPOSMOLYVOS.COM**

BUCKET LIST #59: CAMP WITH HORSES IN MONGOLIA

Traveling along for days at a time with pack horse running alongside, and then making camp, learning out to picket a horse line, hobble their horse, let them  out to graze, fetch them in the mornings to saddle, helping with the packing, and then setting off on a new day, another adventure and another camp somewhere down the trail.

**BOOK A HORSE RIDING HOLIDAY WITH STONE HORSE
MONGOLIA: WWW.STONEHORSEMONGOLIA.COM**

BUCKET LIST #60:
RIDE IN PARADISE

Ride horses in Costa Rica! Join us for a day ride or stay with us on the ranch for a real Adventure in Paradise. The Painted Pony is a family owned guest ranch minutes from Costa Rica's Pacific beaches

BOOK A HORSE RIDING HOLIDAY IN COSTA RICA. VISIT: HTTP://WWW.CASAGUAHORSES.NET

BUCKET LIST #61:
GO ON A CHRISTMAS RIDE

BOOK A HORSE RIDING HOLIDAY IN FRANCE. VISIT: WWW.FRENCHRIDINGHOLIDAYS.CO.UK

Arizona

BUCKET LIST #62:
TACKLE THE GRAND CANYON BY MULE

Try not to look down! This may not be suitable for those scared of heights...

BUCKET LIST #63:
EQUESTRIAN YOGA

India

Yoga is an ancient cultural practice in India and here everyone practises it in different way. Combining Yoga with horses is a beautiful trend and both fit extremely well together. In both Yoga and horse riding we need to practice mindfulness and concentrate on being, breathing and being rooted in the present. We are happy to offer an introduction or a more advanced practise of Yoga on and with horses to our riders on all our Stationary programs.

India

BOOK A HORSE RIDING HOLIDAY IN INDIA. VISIT: HTTP://WWW.PRINCESSTRAILS.COM

"IT'S A LOT LIKE NUTS AND BOLTS, IF THE RIDER'S NUTS, THE HORSE BOLTS!" - NICHOLAS EVANS

BUCKET LIST #64:
ENDURANCE RACE ON CRIOLLOS

Criollos are native to Pampas and are known for their incredible ability to ride for long distances. The Criollos Breeders Associations hosts a 465-mile endurance race. Competitors aim to complete the race in 72 hours, only being able to eat what they find on the trails.

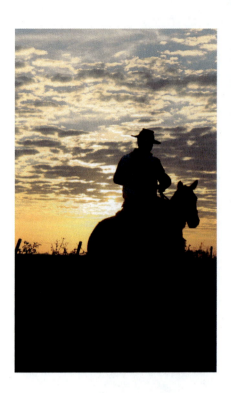

Track Your Miles. Make Memories.

Join Now!

The Ride 1,000 Miles Challenge

BUCKET LIST #65:
CROSS A WILD MONGOLIAN RIVER ON HORSEBACK

The Khentii Mountains of Mongolia, where we ride through the Gorkhi-Terelj and Khan Khentii Special Protected Area, holds the Tuul and the Terelj rivers, and crisscrossed with numerous smaller rivers. We'll cross rivers big and small on a daily basis. Our horses are experts at this and don't hesitate. We'll guide our guests on the best methods and points on crossing rivers and how to do this safely, making is a fun experience.

BOOK A HORSE RIDING HOLIDAY WITH STONE HORSE MONGOLIA: WWW.STONEHORSEMONGOLIA.COM

BUCKET LIST #66:
ZIG ZAG YOUR WAY IN RICE PADDY FIELDS IN ASIA

BUCKET LIST #67:
DISCOVER ANCIENT HISTORY ON HORSEBACK
BOOK A HORSE RIDING HOLIDAY IN GREECE.
VISIT: WWW.IPPOSMOLYVOS.COM

BUCKET LIST #68:
SEE THE NORTHERN LIGHTS ON A RIDE

BUCKET LIST #69:
RIDE HORSES IN GREENLAND

BOOK A HORSE RIDING HOLIDAY IN GREENLAND. VISIT: HTTP://WWW.RIDING-GREENLAND.COM

Romania

Romania

Costa Rica

BUCKET LIST #70:
RIDE IN ROMANIA

BOOK A HORSE RIDING HOLIDAY IN ROMANIA. VISIT: WWW.IZLANDILOVAK.RO

BUCKET LIST #71:
RIDE IN A PLACE WITHOUT FENCES

Leave your stressful life behind and explore a hidden place away from the tourist rush and off the beaten path.

BOOK A HORSE RIDING HOLIDAY IN ROMANIA. VISIT: WWW.IZLANDILOVAK.RO

BUCKET LIST #72:
EXPERIENCE THE RAINFOREST FROM HORSEBACK

BOOK A HORSE RIDING HOLIDAY IN COSTA RICA. VISIT: HTTP://WWW.CASAGUAHORSES.NET

"HORSE SMELL IS THE SAME THE WORLD OVER" — LARA PRIOR-PALMER

BUCKET LIST #73:
EXPERIENCE ANCIENT INCA CIVILIZATION AND ANDEAN CULTURE BY HORSE

Feel the perfect balance between riding and local culture. You dream to be back at the ancient Inca civilization when wandering through the rocky complexes. A professional tour guide explains you everything about the Inca time. Sleeping in local Andean communities and enjoying the exquisite Peruvian cuisine makes your tour complete.

BOOK A HORSE RIDING HOLIDAY IN PERU. VISIT:
WWW.HACIENDADELCHALAN.COM

BUCKET LIST #74:
SEE VIKING RUINS FROM HORSEBACK

The trails are on mountains and can be high up and down. We follow the road of rocks and sometimes go on the sheep trails. There will be no herd of horses with the group, only the horses for the 6 guests and 2 guides.

BOOK A HORSE RIDING HOLIDAY IN GREENLAND. VISIT: HTTP://WWW.RIDING-GREENLAND.COM

BUCKET LIST #75:
RIDE WITH ICEBURGS

BOOK A HORSE RIDING HOLIDAY IN GREENLAND. VISIT: HTTP://WWW.RIDING-GREENLAND.COM

New Zealand

New Zealand

New Zealand

BUCKET LIST #76:
RIDE WITH GLACIERS

We are a boutique multiday horseback adventure company deep in the heart of the southern alps New Zealand. Ride a beautiful horse through glacial rivers, lakes & breathtaking mountain ranges of NZ South Island.

BOOK A HORSE RIDING VACATION IN NEW ZEALAND. VISIT: WWW.ADVENTUREHORSETREKKING.CO.NZ/

BUCKET LIST #77:
HAVE A "DIGITAL DETOX"

Digital detox to refresh your mind as you are enveloped in Papatuanuku "Mother Earth" astounding beauty. Team up with an adventure horse, ride the hidden pack trails through the high mountain peaks of the NZ Southern Alps. Great digital detox, incredible star gazing.

BOOK A HORSE RIDING VACATION IN NEW ZEALAND. VISIT: WWW.ADVENTUREHORSETREKKING.CO.NZ/

THE LORD OF THE RINGS TRILOGY WAS FILMED IN NEW ZEALAND.

DID YOU KNOW?

"IT FEELS GOOD TO BE LOST IN THE RIGHT DIRECTION" – UNKNOWN

"THERE IS ONLY ONE WORD FOR NEW ZEALAND... EPIC."

BEAR GRYLLS

BUCKET LIST #78:
RIDE IN NEW ZEALAND

With breath-taking locations from 2 to 11 day adventures take you far from the tourist routes to explore High Mountain Peaks through the forgotten pack trails threaded through the mountain peaks.

Costa Rica

Costa Rica

Romania

BUCKET LIST #79:
GO ON AN ADVENTURE

BOOK A HORSE RIDING HOLIDAY IN COSTA RICA. VISIT: HTTP://WWW.CASAGUAHORSES.NET

BUCKET LIST #80:
SEE WILDLIFE FROM BETWEEN THE EARS OF A HORSE

BOOK A HORSE RIDING HOLIDAY IN COSTA RICA. VISIT: HTTP://WWW.CASAGUAHORSES.NET

BUCKET LIST #81:
RIDE IN A COUNTRY YOU'VE NEVER HEARD OF BEFORE

BOOK A HORSE RIDING HOLIDAY IN ROMANIA. VISIT: WWW.IZLANDILOVAK.RO

THE WORLD'S BEST DRIVING ROAD IS IN ROMANIA

DID YOU KNOW?

"ON THE BACK OF A HORSE, YOU WILL FIND PARADISE." – STELLA A. WALKER

BUCKET LIST #82:
STAYING OVERNIGHT AT PALACE HOTELS

Riding the Marwari horse is a regal experience, but staying at some of the former palaces and village forts of the Indian maharajas will make it even more special. On our Castle-to-Castle Safari you will arrive each afternoon at another special place. A hunting lodge, a countryside retreat or a village fort, each hotel is unique and will give you a deep insight into Rajasthani history and culture.

BOOK A HORSE RIDING HOLIDAY IN INDIA. VISIT: HTTP://WWW.PRINCESSTRAILS.COM

Use Your Helmet Bag as a Purse

Fly in style and still be able to carry your helmet without it taking up too much space in your checkin bag.

Helpful Travel Tips ——

> ## "I TRAVEL NOT TO GO ANYWHERE, BUT TO GO. I TRAVEL FOR TRAVEL'S SAKE"
>
> *Robert Louis Stevenson*

BUCKET LIST #83:
RIDE THE SILK ROAD

Horses were a symbol of vitality and strength in ancient China. They traveled down this Eurasian trade route to transport goods to other villages. Today, horses still leave hoof prints on the 4,000-mile track through Asia and Europe carrying people to see the historical route.

WHAT TO BRING

- Wide brimmed hat
- Sunscreen
- Helmet
- Long sleeved shirt
- Snacks
- Water
- Extra socks
- Bug spray
- Hard-toed shoes
- Small backpack
- First aid kit
- Rain Slicker
- Compass
- Flashlight
- Map of trail

"A trail ride always frees the mind and opens the heart."

BUCKET LIST #84:

RIDE THROUGH A JUNGLE IN SOUTH AMERICA

HIT THE TRAILS IN SOUTH AMERICA AND RIDE THROUGH ONE OF THE MANY JUNGLES THEY HAVE. YOU WILL GET TO SEE SOME REALLY COOL PLANT AND ANIMAL LIFE IN THIS HUMID CLIMATE. JUST MAKE SURE TO TAKE SOME BUG SPRAY WITH YOU.

SECTION THREE
HORSE BREEDS

FUN TIPS, RESOURCES AND INSPIRATIONAL STORIES:
WWW.EQUESTRIANADVENTURESSES.COM

PRO TIP: TO LEARN ABOUT DIFFERENT RARE HORSE BREEDS, TUNE IN EACH WEEK TO THE EQUESTRIAN ADVENTURESSES PODCAST SHOW AVAILABLE FOR FREE ANYWHERE PODCASTS ARE AVAILABLE. (ITUNES, SPOTIFY, STITCHER, AMAZON MUSIC, AUDIBLE AND OUR WEBSITE: EQUESTRIANADVENTURESSES.COM

EQUESTRIAN ADVENTURESSES
POD CAST

"I CAN MAKE A GENERAL IN FIVE MINUTES, BUT A GOOD HORSE IS HARD TO REPLACE." -ABRAHAM LINCOLN

POINT TO POINT RIDE

We will ride Lusitano, Arabian and PRE trekking horses bred in these mountains and trained by a Gredos horseman whose father still led his cattle along the Transhumance route each spring and autumn.

"Man cannot discover new oceans unless he has the courage to lose sight of the shore" – Andre Gide

BUCKET LIST #85:

RIDE LUSITANOS ON A POINT TO POINT RIDE

An unusual opportunity: this ride in western Spain was created for Imagine Riding by a professional forester, guide and wildlife manager ('Ingeniero de Montes') who was raised in Extremadura.

Intimately acquainted with the landscape and trails of northern and western Spain it will be his pleasure to share his knowledge and expertise with us on the trail.

BUCKET LIST #86:
RIDE A LIPIZZANER

Known for their incredible performances where they literally leap and kick out their hind legs in mid-air, Lipizzaner's are the epitome of strength and power, which makes them valued dressage mounts.

When riding these horses, some may say it feels like floating on a cloud. Their gaits are animated yet gives the rider a nice rocking chair motion- just don't fall asleep while riding.

LIPPIZZANERS ARE THE NATIONAL ANIMAL FOR SLOVENIA

DID YOU KNOW?

BUCKET LIST #87:
RIDE A GAITED HORSE

Paso Fino's, Tennessee Walkers, Icelandic Horses... so many to choose from! If you want a smooth ride, these are the type of horses for you.

BUCKET LIST #88:
RIDE A RARE BREED

How cool would it be to ride and Akhal-teke, a Hackney, or a Sorraia? Each breed will leave your jaw dropped with their unique qualities.

BUCKET LIST #89:
RIDE THE EXOTIC MARWARI HORSE

Experience rural Rajasthan through the unique curly touching ears of Horse India's spirited indigenous Marwari breed horses as they escort you sure-footedly around their desert homeland.

**RIDE A MARWARI HORSE WITH HORSE INDIA.
VISIT: HTTPS://WWW.HORSEINDIA.COM**

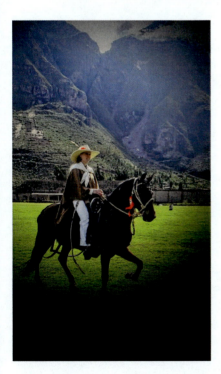

BUCKET LIST #90:
EXPERIENCE RIDING THE SMOOTHEST PERUVIAN PASO HORSES

Enjoy a 6-day trip on the smoothest gated horses of the world. You totally relax and are able to connect with the amazing nature around you. These temperamental, but trustful horses will guide you through the Peruvian Andes.

**BOOK A HORSE RIDING HOLIDAY IN PERU. VISIT:
WWW.HACIENDADELCHALAN.COM**

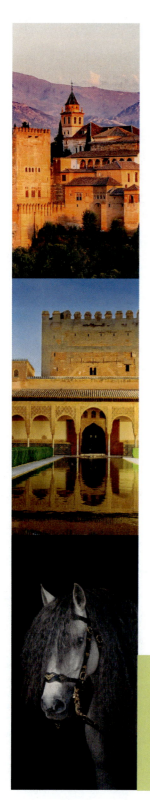

RIDE ANDALUSIANS IN SPAIN

THESE ELEGANT HORSES FROM THE IBERIAN PENISULA COME IN ALL THE MOST BEAUTIFUL COLORS; DAPPLED GRAY WITH A SILVER MANE AND TAIL, CHARCOLE BLACK JUST AS THE NIGHT SKY, AND SILKY CREAM WITH A WHITE POINTS.

RIDING THE PIAFFE, SPANISH WALK & DRESSAGE

Dance the night away on horseback. These Spanish horses have some of the mot exuberant movements that will leave you speechless.

CUISINE AND SPANISH DELICACY

You are going to be hungry after all of that dancing. Go and try some of Spain's mouth-watering cuisine and other traditional foods.

"TRAVEL FAR ENOUGH, YOU MEET YOURSELF."
- DAVID MITCHELL

BUCKET LIST #92:
SEARCH FOR WILD PREZWALSKI'S IN MONGOLIA

The largest herd are located in Hustai National Park in Mongolia. They are sadly on the verge of going extinct, so many of them can be found on reserves.

BUCKET LIST #93:
SPOT A MUSTANG IN THE WILD

Once colonial Spanish mounts, these horses have made their way from domesticated to feral over the years. You can find them roaming wild in the western United States and Canada.

BUCKET LIST #94:
RIDE A HORSE BREED YOU'VE NEVER HEARD OF BEFORE

THE KNABSTRUPPER HORSE BREED WAS FIRST ESTABLISHED IN DENMARK IN 1812.

DID YOU KNOW?

"A GREAT HORSE WILL CHANGE YOUR LIFE. THE TRULY SPECIAL ONES DEFINE IT..." - AUTHOR UNKNOWN

BUCKET LIST #95:
DRIVE A DRAFT

Draft horses are the gentle giants of the horse world and it would be a shame not to get the chance to see them up close and in person!

BUCKET LIST #96:
RIDE AT LEAST 50 DIFFERENT BREEDS OF HORSES

BUCKET LIST #97:
RIDE A HORSE OF EVERY COLOR

BUCKET LIST #98:

RIDE A BREED IN THE COUNTRY THEY WERE FOUNDED

Ride a New Forest Pony in New Forest England, an Icelandic in Iceland... the possibilities are endless!

BUCKET LIST #99:

VISIT THE SHETLAND ISLANDS & GET A PHOTO OF A SHETLAND PONY

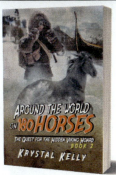

#100

Ride an Arabian in Egypt

Take a trip down sandy roads on these dished-face horses. Go through local villages and banana plantations, site seeing Egyptian culture at its finest. Oh, and don't forget to go see the pyramids!

DID YOU KNOW?

Many Arabians are missing a vertebre, which defines their shorter backs compared to other breeds.

Watch a Thoroughbred Race

It is like thunder as they race down the tracks. These angelic horses will leave goosebumps on your arms as they cross the finish line. They are said to have so much heart and are like big puppy dogs.

DID YOU KNOW?

Two-year-old filly, Winning Brew, broke the world record for the highest race speed in 2008 at 43.5 mph in 20.57 seconds.

#102

Work Cattle on a Quarter Horse

Grab your rope and take a trip out to Montana. Quarter Horses are known for their cattle working abilities and gentle disposition even though they can be a little stubborn at time... They probably just get it from the cows.

DID YOU KNOW?

These horses can outrun other breeds in a quarter of a mile; hence their name.

#103

Ride a Fjord in Norway

Crystal clear water running down a narrow inlet waterway, pressed in-between two steep cliffs that are filled with greenery; you are looking at a fjord. This is the native land to the breed and where they received their name.

DID YOU KNOW?

Viking once used these horses in battle. They valued their sturdy structure and bravery.

SECTION FOUR
RIDER TRAINING & EDUCATION

**FUN TIPS, RESOURCES AND INSPIRATIONAL STORIES:
WWW.EQUESTRIANADVENTURESSES.COM**

Track Your Miles. Make Memories.

Join Now!

The Ride 1,000 Miles Challenge

PRO TIP: SIGN UP FOR THE VIRTUAL ENDURANCE "RIDE 1,000 MILE CHALLENGE" AND ENJOY A VIRTUAL EVENT WITH FELLOW CHALLENGER PARTICIPANTS. WIN PRIZES, HAVE ADVENTURES WITH YOUR HORSE, AND COLLECT COOL BADGES!

WORKSHOP.EQUESTRIANADVENTURESSES.COM/1000-MILE-CHALLENGE

"IF YOU PERSEVERE LONG ENOUGH, IF YOU DO THE RIGHT THINGS LONG ENOUGH, THE RIGHT THINGS WILL HAPPEN." - IAN MILLER

The International Equestrian Rider Training Scale

Beginner: Forest Green

Level 1:
Begin "Following Horse's" Motions
Introduction to Rider Balance in walk trot and canter

Beginner: Mint Green

Level 2:
Master "Following Horse's" Motions
Master Rider Balance in walk trot and canter

Intermediate: Navy Blue

Level 3:
Begin Transition to "Horse Following YOUR Motion"
Introduction to Helping Your Horse's Balance

Level 4:
Master "Horse Following YOUR Motion" on multiple horses + successfully help horse's balance
Begin Developing of Timing & Coordination of Aids

Intermediate: Arctic Blue

Level 5:
Master Timing & Coordination of Aids
Moving Up Your Discipline Specific Goals & Levels

Advanced: Medallion Gold

BUCKET LIST #104:
WORK THROUGH THE LEVELS WITH THE INTERNATIONAL EQUESTRIAN

More information about the Training Scale on the website:
www.theinternationalequestrian.com

BUCKET LIST #105:
COMPETE IN A HORSE SHOW

Not just in your sport or discipline... but a new one!

BUCKET LIST #106:
TRY A DIFFERENT DISCIPLINE

Western, side-saddle, dressage, endurance or maybe sit in a gaucho saddle! Sign up for a polo lesson or take an archery class.

RIDE 1,000 MILES ON A SINGLE HORSE IN 1 YEAR

Join the Ride 1,000 Miles Challenge:
www.equestrianadventuresses.com

BUCKET LIST #108:

RIDE 1,000 MILES ON MULTIPLE HORSES

BUCKET LIST #109:

PARTICIPATE IN A "RIDE & TIE"

This fun sport combines riding, running. This is a team sport based on endurance and strategy.

BUCKET LIST #110:
CROSS TRAIN USING THE GUIDED AUDIO RIDING LESSONS

Step By Step Riding Instruction you can listen to while you ride straight from your phone. More information on the website: www.theinternationalequestrian.com

BUCKET LIST #111:
RIDE IN A SADDLE YOU'VE NEVER TRIED BEFORE

What our Guided Audio Riding Lesson students are saying...

"This is just what I need! I've been a life long rider. Having guided lessons where I can focus on Krystal's calm and knowledgeable voice coming through the ear buds helps me to stay focused on something other than the "what if's" in my head. I'm starting to breathe and relax and channel my inner confident rider again!" -Eline

www.theinternationalequestrian.com

Erica
7m · 🌐

Today while listening to Krystal and doing the rein back lesson, she is saying to take a deep breath and she does it......and he stopped from her deep breath 😂

BUCKET LIST #112:

HAVE A PROFESSIONAL CREATE A CUSTOM TRAINING PLAN FOR YOU

www.theinternationalequestrian.com

See what our "Sticky Butt Bootcampers" are saying...

Kathie
1h · 🌐

I have a Sticky Butt shout out!! I sent my horse off to my old trainer and had a lesson on him today with her (I haven't ridden with her in a year and a half and didn't ride in between) she used to come to me so I never rode around anyone, I was so nervous riding with all the Grand Prix girls so I couldn't focus. My trainer said she couldn't believe how much my balance and seat have improved. I used to balance on my reins and now she had to tell me to tighten them. Of course I told her it was the sticky butt program!! 🤯😀

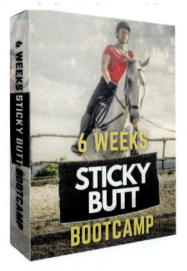 

BUCKET LIST #113:
GET A "STICKY BUTT"
www.theinternationalequestrian.com

BUCKET LIST #114:
LEARN TO SPEAK THE HORSE LANGUAGE
www.theinternationalequestrian.com

SECTION FIVE
ARTS + CHARITABLE

FUN TIPS, RESOURCES AND INSPIRATIONAL STORIES:
WWW.EQUESTRIANADVENTURESSES.COM

PRO TIP: WHEN BOOKING A HORSE TOUR ABROAD OR TRAVELING TO ANOTHER COUNTRY, CHECK WITH THE LOCAL STABLES OR CHARITIES IF YOU CAN BRING ANYTHING FROM HOME THAT MIGHT HELP THEIR CAUSE. (EXAMPLE: EXTRA SNAFFLE BITS, SADDLE PADS, ETC.) OFTEN TIMES THESE ITEMS ARE NOT EASILY AVAILABLE IN THIRD WORLD COUNTRIES AND A FEW SADDLE PAD DONATIONS GOES A LONG WAY!

"I CALL HORSES 'DIVINE MIRRORS.' THEY REFLECT BACK THE EMOTIONS YOU PUT IN. IF YOU PUT IN LOVE AND RESPECT AND KINDNESS AND CURIOSITY, THE HORSE WILL RETURN THAT." - ALLAN HAMILTON

BUCKET LIST #115:
SEE THE "KELPIES" IN SCOTLAND

Kelpies in Scottish legends are aquatic spirits. These beautiful sculptures are 30 meters high and located in Falkirk, Scotland.

BUCKET LIST #116:
VISIT THE NATIONAL HORSE RACING MUSEUM IN ENGLAND

Learn about history, such as the first recorded race that took place in Newmarket, see art pieces, paintings, sculptures awards and more.

⚡ **Pro Tip:** Visit "The Tack Room" for a drink after exploring the museum.

BUCKET LIST #117:
VISIT THE COWBOY MUSEUM IN OKLAHOMA

Learn about the Pony Express, Cowboys, and the "Sante Fe Trail" and it's heritage.

BUCKET LIST #118:
SEE THE ORIGINAL PAINTING OF NAPOLEON CROSSING THE ALPS

BUCKET LIST #119:
VISIT THE INTERNATIONAL MUSEUM OF THE HORSE IN KENTUCKY

Walk through history with horses, see live shows, saddle up and go for a trail ride, or stay at the campsite and enjoy the facilities. There is plenty to see and do at the Horse Musuem in Kentucky!

BUCKET LIST #120:
VISIT A LOCAL HORSE RESCUE & VOLUNTEER FOR THE DAY

BUCKET LIST #121:
DONATE TO AN INTERNATIONAL HORSE CHARITY

Some recommendations:
The Donkey Sanctuary (Ireland)
Horse Feathers Equine Center (Oklahoma)
Horses of Gili (Indonesia, Gili Islands)
World Horse Welfare
The Ukrainian Equestrian Federation Charity Foundation

BUCKET LIST #122:
HAVE A PROFESSIONAL PAINTING / DRAWING MADE OF YOUR HORSE

BUCKET LIST #123:
PHOTOSHOOT WITH HORSES

Dress up in costumes, hire a professional equine photographer and either take amazing photos with your own horse or beautiful Andalusians, Fresians and more. Be a knight or a lady. Dress like an elf from Lord of the Rings or any of your favorite characters from movies and books.

BUCKET LIST #124:
SEE THE HIT PLAY "WAR HORSE"

BUCKET LIST #125:
RIDE WITH A CONSCIENCE - BIT DONATION SCHEME

Give something back to the indigenous equestrian community of Rajasthan by distributing smooth snaffle bits to rural village horse owners during your ride through with Horse India who actively support and promote the Bit Donation Scheme.

FOR MORE INFO ON THE BIT DONATION SCHEME WITH HORSE INDIA VISIT: HTTPS://WWW.HORSEINDIA.COM

JOIN THE CHALLENGE! VISIT: WWW.THEINTERNATIONALEQUESTRIAN.COM

You don't
need magic
to disappear.
All you need is
a destination.

—

CARA JANE RENNER
travel blogger

Travel Essentials

Don't forget these items while traveling!

Helmet

Bring your own helmet (pack it in a helmet bag and use it as a purse!)

Vitamin C

Vitamin to keep you healthy and keep you from getting ill.

Sunscreen

To protect your skin from the UV lights

Tumbler

No more plastic water bottles! Use a tumbler

Helpful Travel Tips ——

ABOUT THE AUTHORS

Krystal Kelly

Krystal Kelly is founder of Equestrian Adventuresses and an avid traveler on a quest to visit every country in the world. She left her home in California at the age of 21 to work abroad with top show jumping horses. She has since worked in over 20 countries with horses including Egypt, India, Romania, and many others. In 2016 she met her husband in Azerbaijan while driving a crappy car from England to Mongolia and back. Her love of adventurous travel has led her to the farthest corners of the Earth to film for the Equestrian Adventuresses Documentary series, available on Amazon Prime, the Equus Film Channel and the Equestrian Adventuresses web- site. She enjoys bringing her husband along for the ride to capture the beauty on film.

www.equestrianadventuresses.com

ABOUT THE AUTHORS

Georgia Smith

Traveller and horse-lover at heart, Georgia Smith attends Middle Tennessee State University in pursuits of a Journalism degree. After college, she aims to become a travel journalist while still focusing on her equine roots. Georgia grew up showing Quarter Horses in western all-around events and involved herself in the local 4-H equine program where she competed in horse judging and won nationals in 2017. Her goal is to share her passion of storytelling through her writings, photography, and other creative media while exploring different cultures and having adventures around the world. In her free time, Georgia loves to be outdoors and spend time with her beloved friends and family.

Equestrian Adventuresses

Travel Planner

Today's
Plan _____

DSTN: _____ NO: _____

To do	Notes

Dinner :

Breakfast :

Lunch :

Exercise

Equestrian Adventuresses

Travel Planner

Today's Plan _____

DSTN: _____. NO: _____

To do	Notes

Dinner :

Breakfast :

Lunch :

Exercise

Equestrian Adventuresses

Travel Planner

Today's **Plan** _____

DSTN: _____ NO: _____

To do	Notes

Dinner :

Breakfast :

Lunch :

Exercise

Equestrian Adventuresses

Travel Planner

Today's **Plan** _____

DSTN: _____. NO:_____

To do

Notes

Dinner :

Breakfast :

Lunch :

Exercise

Equestrian Adventuresses

Travel Planner

Today's Plan _____

DSTN: _____ NO: _____

To do	Notes

Dinner :

Breakfast :

Lunch :

Exercise

Made in the USA
Las Vegas, NV
07 December 2023

82258494R00062